The Story of Our Holidays

EASTER

Joanna Ponto

Enslow Publishing
101 W. 23rd Street
Suite 240
New York, NY 10011
USA

enslow.com

Published in 2016 by Enslow Publishing, LLC.
101 W. 23rd Street, Suite 240, New York, NY 10011

Library of Congress Cataloging-in-Publication Data

Names: Ponto, Joanna.
Title: Easter / Joanna Ponto.
Description: New York : Enslow Publishing, 2016 | Series: The story of our holidays | Includes index.
Identifiers: ISBN 9780766074705 (pbk.) | ISBN 9780766074644 (6 pack) | ISBN 9780766074583
  (library bound)
Subjects: LCSH: Easter—Juvenile literature.
Classification: LCC GT4935.P66 2016 | DDC 394.2'68283—dc23

Printed in the United States of America

To Our Readers: We have done our best to make sure all website addresses in this book were active and
appropriate when we went to press. However, the author and the publisher have no control over and
assume no liability for the material available on those websites or on any websites they may link to.
Any comments or suggestions can be sent by e-mail to customerservice@enslow.com.

Portions of this book originally appeared in the book *Easter: Parades, Chocolates, and Celebration.*

Contents

Many children look forward to meeting the Easter Bunny.

4

Chapter 1

Hopping Bunnies and Hopeful Celebrations

Spring is almost here. You are at the mall with your family. You do not see it coming, but you look up and there it is. A large white furry rabbit is headed your way. This bunny must be about six feet tall. Maybe it is wearing blue overalls and cowboy boots. The rabbit carries a basket of brightly colored eggs. It gives out jellybeans and small chocolate bunnies to children passing by.

Everyone knows the rabbit is not real. (Everyone who is older than three, that is.) It is a person in a costume. But it is not a Halloween costume. The person in the rabbit suit is pretending to be the Easter Bunny. You see lots of Easter Bunnies this time of year. It is a sign that Easter is almost here.

A Special Festival

Easter is a special festival. It is a time for hope and rejoicing. Many children are given Easter baskets filled with treats. They go on Easter egg hunts. Families come together. They enjoy wonderful Easter dinners.

Easter is also a religious holiday. It is an important day for Christians. Christians believe that Jesus is the son of God. They also believe that after Jesus died, he came back to life. This is known as the Resurrection.

Christians believe that Jesus gives his followers hope. On Easter, Christians celebrate Jesus's Resurrection. They also celebrate the promise of being with Jesus forever in Heaven.

A Symbol of Spring

Bunnies are a symbol of spring. There is an old German story about the Easter Bunny. In the story, a woman hid colorful Easter eggs outdoors. Her children went out to hunt for them. Just then, a rabbit hopped by. The children thought the rabbit brought the eggs. After that, parents began telling their children that every year the Easter Bunny brings beautifully colored eggs.

Painting Easter eggs is a common tradition that many families enjoy together.

Christians have celebrated Easter since early times. It is the oldest Christian festival. It is the most important, as well. This is a book about Easter and how people make the holiday special.

Chapter 2

The Easter Story

Easter is a celebration of spring. Signs of new life are everywhere. Green grass and bright flowers sprout. Birds sing in the trees.

The Story of Jesus

Jesus lived more than two thousand years ago. He was a Jew from the area now known as Israel.

Some people thought Jesus was God's son. He preached to many people and tried to teach them how to live. Some said he performed miracles.

Many people began to follow Jesus. He had twelve special followers known as the Apostles. They helped Jesus tell people about what he believed.

In time, more people heard about Jesus. Crowds gathered wherever he went. These people loved and respected Jesus. For years, they had waited for God to send someone to save them. They believed that it was Jesus. They thought of him as a messiah or king.

Palm Sunday

Jesus came to the city of Jerusalem riding on a donkey. The people cheered as he passed. They waved palm branches to greet him. This was usually done to welcome kings and queens.

By then, many people looked up to Jesus. But some thought that Jesus was becoming too powerful. This was especially true of the Romans who ruled then.

Dawn: The Start of a New Day

We are not sure where the word "Easter" comes from, but it may be connected to spring festivals. Many years ago, people prayed to a spring goddess. Her name was Eastre. Other people say there was a spring festival called Eastre. Still others claim that the name comes from the German word *eostarun*, which means "dawn." Dawn is the start of a new day. Easter marks the start of a new season. It is the season of new growth.

Worshipers light candles during an Easter service at the Church of the Holy Sepulchre in Jerusalem, Israel.

While in Jerusalem, Jesus celebrated the Jewish festival of Passover. He ate Passover supper with the Apostles. Later, he led them to a large garden outside the city. They were to spend the night there. But just before morning, the Roman soldiers came and arrested Jesus.

A hearing was held. The Romans said he had broken their laws. Jesus was found guilty and sentenced to die.

Death on the Cross

The next day, the Romans nailed Jesus to a cross. At that time, many people were killed that way.

Jesus died on the cross later that day. Before sundown, some of Jesus's followers came and took his body to a stone tomb. Then they rolled a large stone in front of it to cover the opening.

Two days passed. On the morning of the third day, some of Jesus's followers went back to the tomb. The stone had been rolled away. Jesus's body was gone.

Alive!

Jesus had told his followers that he would rise from the dead. Christians celebrate the Resurrection of Jesus as the day on which they believe he came back to life and left his tomb.

Jesus rose from the dead. This is why Easter is celebrated.

Over the next forty days, Jesus appeared before his disciples and told them to go out and spread his teachings. This is how Christianity began. Today there are millions of Christians around the world.

Chapter 3

A Season of Celebrations

Some holidays last only a day. But Easter is more than Easter Sunday. There is also an Easter season.

Christians celebrate Easter every spring. But unlike Christmas, Easter is not always on the same date. Easter may fall on any Sunday between March 22 and April 25. Whatever the date, Christians celebrate. It is a day to rejoice.

Lent

Lent always begins on a Wednesday. This is known as Ash Wednesday. Large numbers of Christians go to church on Ash Wednesday. Some have a dab of ash placed on their foreheads. This is to remind them to begin Lent with a humble spirit.

The first part of this season is Lent. Holy Week is the last week of Lent. Many churches have special services all seven days. Holy Week reminds Christians of the week of Jesus's death and Resurrection.

The first day of Holy Week is Palm Sunday. Palm Sunday celebrates Jesus's ride into Jerusalem. Today some churches give out palm fronds, or leaves, on Palm Sunday. Often the fronds are made into the shape of a cross.

Many churches celebrate Palm Sunday by giving out palms.

Another important day during Holy Week is Maundy Thursday. It is also known as Holy Thursday. That night, Jesus and his Apostles shared Passover supper. The dinner has become known as the Last Supper because it was Jesus's last meal.

The Friday of Holy Week is called Good Friday. Jesus died on the cross that day. It is a sad time. Some churches hold three-hour services on Good Friday. There are sermons about Jesus's last words on the cross.

Easter Sunday

Easter Sunday is the last day of Holy Week. Christians celebrate Jesus's Resurrection. In early times, people believed the Easter

Forty Days of Lent

Lent lasts for forty days. During Lent, Christians prepare for Easter. They think about their sins. They seek forgiveness. Years ago, Christians did this by fasting. Fasting means not eating or eating very little. For hundreds of years, Christians gave up meat, eggs, cheese, and butter during Lent. Today Christians often give up one thing they really like.

Some Christians attend a sunrise service on Easter Sunday.

sunrise was special. They thought the sun danced up to the sky that morning. They would gather outdoors to see it.

Today many churches have Easter sunrise services. The early light reminds Christians of Jesus. They call Jesus the light of the world.

Chapter 4

Symbols of Spring and Easter

Many symbols remind us of Easter. A symbol is something that stands for something else. Colored eggs and bunnies are two well-known Easter symbols. We expect to see these at Easter. The holiday would not seem complete without them.

But some Easter symbols were used even before Easter. They were used in spring festivals. Over time, parts of these festivals became mixed with Easter celebrations. So today we think of them as Easter symbols.

Easter eggs are often brightly colored.

Colored Eggs

The egg is a symbol of new life. For thousands of years, eggs were part of many spring festivals. People would color eggs. They would give these to one another.

Flowers

Easter lilies are tall, sweet-smelling plants. They have large white blossoms that are shaped like trumpets. The Easter lily is an Easter symbol because of the shape of its flowers. They stand for trumpets to announce Jesus's Resurrection. The Easter lily's white color stands for purity.

Lambs

For thousands of years, lambs were killed or sacrificed for the gods. They were used as an offering or gift. At Easter, the lamb stands for Jesus. Christians sometimes call

Lambs are a common symbol of spring.

Good Luck Buns

Hot cross buns have a cross on top made of white icing. Hot cross buns were made for years before Easter. But they became an Easter symbol. In early times, people thought these buns brought good luck. They would hang a hot cross bun from their ceiling to protect their home. Sailors often took these buns out to sea with them. They hoped the buns would keep them safe during storms at sea.

Jesus the lamb of God. They believe that Jesus sacrificed himself on the cross. He did this so God would forgive the sins of the world.

Light

Candles are lit during Easter. Their flame stands for Jesus's light. Light is also a symbol of hope and new life.

Colors of Easter

Some colors make us think of Easter. These are usually white, yellow, purple, and green. White stands for purity. Yellow is for sunlight. It also stands for the light Jesus brought to the world. Purple is the color of mourning. It stands for the sorrow felt over Jesus's death. Green is the color of nature. It stands for spring and rebirth.

Chapter 5

Easter's Celebrations

Easter Sunday is a time of joy. It is also a day to celebrate. Many Christians go to church that day. On Easter morning, church bells ring out across the nation. Churches are often decorated for Easter. They may be filled with Easter lilies.

At times, Christians go to Easter sunrise services. Sunrise services are usually held outdoors. Some are in parks or on beaches. Others are on hilltops. People get together where they feel close to God. As the sun comes up, they pray and sing. They listen to sermons. Afterward some groups have a special Easter breakfast.

People usually look their best. Many adults and children wear new clothes on Easter. Women and girls may have fancy hats. These are sometimes called Easter bonnets.

Festivals of Easter

On Easter, many people go to holiday festivals. Easter festivals have games and music. There are good things to eat. Actors dressed as Easter bunnies give out candy. There may be Easter bonnet contests. Prizes may be given for the largest, smallest, prettiest, and funniest hats.

Family Time

Other people plan a large Easter meal later in the day. Often it is a wonderful feast. Lamb or ham is served. There may be mint jelly, potatoes, candied carrots, and a wide choice of salads. A white cake baked in the shape of a lamb is a popular Easter dessert. Children are also given Easter cookies or cupcakes. These may be shaped like lambs, bunnies, or angels.

Many Christian families try to be together on Easter. They want to spend this special day with their relatives. Some people travel hundreds of miles to do this.

Easter Treats

Easter is especially wonderful for children. In some families, young people receive Easter baskets. These are baskets filled with treats.

Can you eat a whole chocolate bunny?

Most have lots of candy. Every Easter, sixty million chocolate rabbits are eaten. So are more than six hundred million small marshmallow chicks. Marshmallow eggs and bunnies are popular Easter sweets, as well.

Jellybeans are another favorite Easter candy. These are sometimes called jelly eggs. They look like tiny Easter eggs. Americans eat about fifteen million jelly beans every Easter. What if all these jelly beans were placed end to end? They could circle the earth three times!

Easter Carrot Cupcakes*

Cupcake Ingredients:

2 cups (400 g) white sugar
¾ cup (180 mL) vegetable oil
3 eggs
1 teaspoon (5 mL) vanilla
  extract
¾ cup (180 mL) buttermilk
  or half and half
2 cups (300 g) grated carrots
1 cup (150 g) flaked coconut
½ cup (120 mL) applesauce
2 cups (240 g) all-purpose
  flour
2 teaspoons (10 mL) baking
  soda
2 teaspoons (10 mL)
  ground cinnamon
1 teaspoon (5 mL) ground
  nutmeg
1 teaspoon (5 mL) salt
1 cup (150 g) chopped
  walnuts or pecans
  (optional)

Cupcake Directions:

1. Preheat oven to 350°F (175°C) Lay cupcake wrappers into muffin tin, spraying lightly with nonstick cooking oil.
2. In a large bowl combine sugar, oil, eggs, vanilla, and buttermilk. Stir in carrots, coconut, vanilla, and applesauce.
3. In a separate bowl, combine flour, baking soda, spices, and salt. Gently sift into wet ingredients. This prevents any clumps or bubbles in the batter. Stir in chopped nuts if desired.
4. Spoon batter into cupcake wrappers, until they're about ¾ full (about 3 heaping tablespoons).
5. Bake for 30 minutes or until a toothpick inserted into cake comes out clean. Set aside to cool.

Cream Cheese Frosting Ingredients:

½ cup (120 g) butter, softened
1 (8-ounce) (226 g) package cream
  cheese
1 teaspoon (5 mL) vanilla extract
4 cups (400 g) confectioners' sugar

Frosting Directions:

1. In a medium mixing bowl, combine butter, cream cheese, and vanilla. Beat on high until smooth.
2. Slowly stir in the confectioner's sugar.
3. Frost the cupcakes when they're cool. Eat and enjoy!

* Adult supervision required.

Chapter 6

All Kinds of Celebrations!

Easter baskets can be filled with all sorts of fun things. Some have both small toys and candy. Others may be based on a child's interests. An Easter basket can have just baseball cards and a baseball in it, or it may be filled with art supplies. But one thing is certain. An Easter basket is always a welcome gift.

Celebrations Everywhere

People celebrate Easter in many different ways. Stores decorate for Easter. Libraries display Easter books. Sometimes someone in a bunny suit even stops by.

Museums display solid gold Easter eggs. Some are decorated with brightly colored jewels. These can be worth millions of dollars!

These jeweled eggs are called fabregè (fab-re-jay).

School Celebrations

Most schools share in the holiday fun. Classrooms are decorated. There may be special holiday craft programs. Students make Easter baskets out of cardboard, paint, and ribbons. They make small bunnies out of marshmallows and toothpicks.

Students also make Easter cards. They give these to their friends, teachers, and families. Easter cards are the second most common cards sent by young people. Only Valentine's Day cards outnumber them!

Some schools close on Good Friday. Schools may be closed on Easter Monday, as well. That is the Monday after Easter Sunday.

Before Easter many children like to color Easter eggs. Sometimes families do this together. Friends dye eggs together, too.

Some Easter eggs are beautiful. They have fancy designs in many colors. At times, people hang their nicest eggs on the branches of small trees. These are indoor trees. People also hang large plastic eggs on outdoor trees.

Egg Hunts and Rolls

Easter eggs are used in other fun ways, too. Easter egg hunts are common in the United States. In an Easter egg hunt, children try to find hidden Easter eggs. Often the child with the most eggs wins a prize.

Perhaps the best known Easter egg hunt is held at the White House South Lawn. The president of the United States lives in the White House. Quite a few young Americans

Easter Gardens

Botanical gardens are places where special plants are grown and cared for. Visitors come to see the rare and often beautiful plants there. Every Easter, many gardens have children's activities. The young people may be given seeds to plant in pots. At home, they water and watch over their plants. Soon the plants begin to grow. It is a wonderful way to celebrate both Easter and spring.

visit for the Easter activities, such as the egg roll, when they race by pushing an egg with a spoon.

Special guests from other lands are there, too. They tell how Easter is celebrated in their countries. Visitors may also get to see the White House egg collection. It is made up of eggs decorated by American artists. There is one egg from an artist from each of the fifty states.

President Barack Obama cheers on one of the younger children having fun at the White House Easter Egg Roll.

Easter egg hunts are also held all over. Students at the Blind Children's Learning Center in Los Angeles, California, have a special one. At that hunt, tiny beepers are placed in plastic eggs. These give off a small beeping sound. Children who are blind or do not see well use their ears instead of their eyes to find the eggs.

Parades!

The Easter holiday is also well known for parades. One of the most famous Easter parades is in New York City. It takes place every Easter Sunday.

New York City's Easter parade began many years ago. Then people strolled down Fifth Avenue after church. They were dressed in their best Easter clothes. Women wore fabulous hats. It was really a fashion parade.

Today the parade is no longer about fashion. Instead it is a wild and wacky parade. People wear funny hats and crazy costumes.

Sharing

Many people believe it is important to share with others on Easter. Easter food drives are common. Food is donated and given to people in need.

These are just some of the ways people celebrate Easter. You may know other ways. It is easy to enjoy Easter and have fun. But it is also important to keep the spirit of Easter alive. That means bringing hope and joy to whatever you do on that special holiday.

Easter Craft

Here's how to make a cute decoration for Easter.

egg carton
yellow pom-poms (different sizes)
glue
orange construction paper
scissors
markers

Directions:

1. Cut the egg cartons in half. Put one half aside.

2. Glue one large pom-pom into each of the six egg holes to form the body of each chick.

3. Glue a smaller pom-pom on top of each large pom-pom. Let dry.

4. Cut six small diamond shapes from the orange construction paper. Fold each diamond in half to make six beaks. Glue them to the front of each small pom-pom. Let dry.

5. Use a marker to make eyes on each chick.

Baby Chicks

*Safety Note: Be sure to ask for
help from an adult, if needed,
to complete this project.

Glossary

Apostles—Jesus's twelve followers who helped spread his teachings.

disciple—A person who helps spread the teaching of another.

fasting—Not eating or eating very little.

festival—A time of celebration.

humble—Not bold or proud.

mourning—The sorrow felt over someone's death.

Passover—A holiday that celebrates the Jews' freedom from slavery in Egypt.

Resurrection—Jesus's return to life after dying on the cross.

sacrifice—Something killed as an offering to a god.

sermon—A religious speech by a priest, minister, or rabbi.

Easter bonnets are a common tradition. There's even a song about them!

Learn More

Books

Cosson, M.J., and Elisa Chavarri. *Easter Traditions Around the World* (World Traditions). Mankato, MN: The Child's World, 2013.

Dateno, Maria Grace, and Paul Cunningham. *Discovery at Dawn* (Gospel Time Trekkers #6). Boston, MA: Pauline Books and Media, 2014.

Owen, Ruth. *Easter Sweets and Treats.* New York: Windmill Books, 2012.

Rau, Dana Meachen, and Kathleen Petelinsek. *Decorating Eggs* (How-To Library). Ann Arbor, MI: Cherry Lake Pub., 2013.

Websites

Easter
history.com/topics/holidays/history-of-easter
Learn more about Easter with facts and videos.

Easter
theholidayspot.com/easter
Visit this website for Easter history, poems, crafts, and more.

Why Do We Celebrate Easter? Fun Easter Facts for Kids
kidsplayandcreate.com/why-do-we-celebrate-easter-fun-easter-facts-for-kids
Check out this fun site for more interesting facts about Easter.

Index